Table of Contents

Chapter 1: Introduction

In this book, Dog Grooming: Your Definitive Guide to DIY Dog Grooming for Fun & Profit, you will be learning all about dog grooming.

Here, some of the things you can learn are:

- The basics of dog grooming (such as hair grooming and ear care)
- Essential grooming tools
- How to handle dogs with anxiety
- Dog coat care
- Dog grooming styles
- Issues with your dog's fur
- Dog dental care
- Extreme grooming makeover

This book discusses dog grooming for dogs of all sorts – both for fun and for profit. Here, you can read about dog grooming lessons for dogs regardless of age, temperament, or breed.

Dog grooming is essential, and it goes beyond the idea of "beautifying" a dog. It's about caring for a dog's health, too, and allowing him to live a better quality of life.

And, if you think that grooming your dog is rather costly and time-consuming, this book can help change your mind. In a matter of time and a series of lessons, you'll get yourself a well-groomed and picture-perfect dog!

And, if you don't know where to start, let this book lend you a hand. You can handle it all by yourself, too. Hiring a professional dog groomer is not necessary. Dog grooming can be a DIY project. After all (and as the subtitle says), this is a "definitive guide to DIY dog grooming."

Downloading this book was the right choice. I hope you enjoy reading through the 11-chapter compilation.

Chapter 2: Dog Grooming - The Basics

Dog grooming is essential if you're a dog parent. And, whether for fun or for profit, you should groom your dog regularly.

Beyond the fact that it makes your dog attractive, dog grooming is also beneficial to your dog's health. It promotes good hygiene. And, not only does it help you recognize different signs of potential health problems, but it also helps prevent the development of these potential health problems.

With regular and proper dog grooming, parasite-related infections, allergies, and poor nutrition are some of the avoidable problems.

Hair Grooming: Recommended Haircuts & Guidelines

A healthy and a shiny coat, minimal hair shedding, and minimal hair build-up (or none at all) are few advantages of grooming your dog's hair. To groom your dog, you need to give him an appropriate haircut, and then brush his hair.

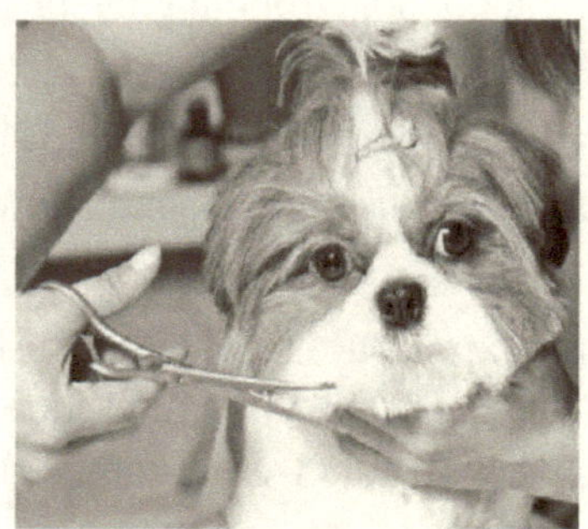

First, you need to give him a haircut. Any style would be okay, so long as it is manageable and doesn't put excessive weight on him.

Here are some recommended haircuts:

- **Continental Cut**
    - Short clippings of hind legs
    - Meant to create a "front heavy" effect

- **English Saddle**
    - Best for Irish Water Spaniels, Poodles and Poodle breeds and mixes, and dogs with thick and curly hair
    - Meant to create "pom-poms" or distinct areas of fur with long fur on the rest of the body parts (except in the legs, tail, and back)
    - Very short clippings in feet, neck, and face

- **Topknot**
    - Best for the Shih Tzu breed, Yorkshire Terriers, and dogs with long hair
    - Meant to keep hair neat and tidy above the dogs' head
    - Bunching and tying only; no clipping required

- **Puppy Cut**
    - Short clippings in feet, neck, hair, and base (of tail) with long and dense fur on the rest of the body parts
    - Meant to complement dogs' form

- **Cords**
    - Best for Pulik, Komondork, and dogs with distinctive thick coats
    - Meant to protect dogs from extreme temperature and harsh natural elements
    - Similar to dreadlocks; with twists and twines

- **Lion Cut**
    - Best for Chow Chows, Pomeranians, and short dogs with dense, curled fur

– Allows dogs to work in a shallow body of water without their coat weighing them down

– Emulates a mane's appearance; short-clipped body with long and dense fur around neck and head

Once he gets the appropriate haircut, it's time to commit to brushing his hair. This prevents tangles and matting.

Usually, a dog likes the idea of a dog parent brushing their hair. So, if he doesn't rebel when you bring him close to you so you could brush his hair, you may take it as a hint that your dog wants you to continue what you're doing.

Remember to brush your dog's hair regularly depending on the kind of hair that he has. Be mindful of these guidelines:

- Short-haired dogs (such as Basenjis, Weimaraners, and Beagles) can go weeks without brushing.

- Medium-haired dogs should be brushed weekly.

- Long-haired and thick-coated dogs (such as Malamutes, and Samoyeds) should be brushed daily.

In addition, not only will it improve your dog's hair, regular brushing also fosters trust. Your dog will start trusting you even more.

If he starts to look forward to brushing sessions, it's a sign he likes his hair getting brushed. This, in turn, will help in other dog grooming activities. Just like brushing, he will start to warm up to other activities.

Bathing Your Dog

And, like in the case of most dog breeds (short-haired breeds, medium-haired breeds, and long-haired breeds) and those with water-repellent coats (such as Great Pyrnees and Golden Retrievers), you should bathe your dog once monthly – unless otherwise advised by attending veterinary dermatologists. Doing so reduces scratching and itching, prevents the development of skin diseases, and generally, cleanses your dog.

Here are some dog bathing tips:

- Before you bathe your dog, it's recommended to brush his hair. Doing so lessens the chances of dealing with tangles and mats.

- Don't bathe your dog (with normal skin) too often as this can cause his skin to get dry or irritated. As mentioned, about once a month is enough, but there are appropriate reasons (for example, he gets dirty frequently, he has an oily coat, or he smells) to bathe him more often, it is recommended to use a moisturizing or soap-free shampoo for dogs.

- Use a dog-friendly shampoo. Avoid shampoos that were created for people (even babies) since the two kinds of shampoos have different pH levels (or measures of acidity).

- Don't let water enter your dog's ears as this will leave them smelling unpleasantly afterwards and he can develop ear infections of sorts. You can temporarily place a piece of cotton.

- Use lukewarm water to prevent chances of burning a dog's sensitive skin.

- Always rinse well after bathing. Leftover soap can cause skin irritation.

Tricks When Trimming Your Dog's Nails

A dog that panics at the idea of nail-trimming sessions is normal dog behavior, especially if he's had a relevant traumatic experience. The minute you show him a nail clipper, he is likely to get away from you as fast as he can.

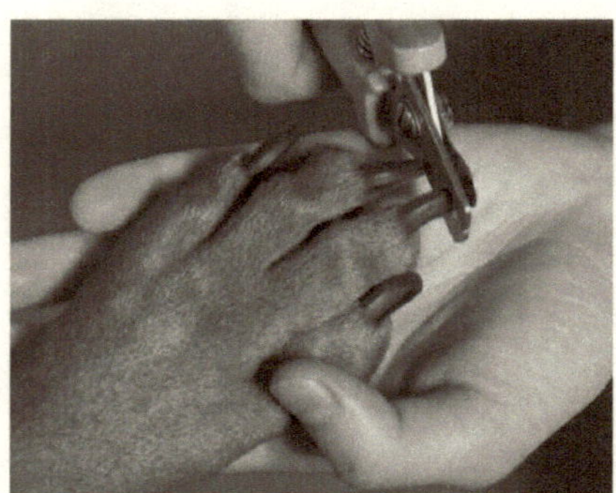

Sure, clipping your dog's nails leads to lots of anxiety – both for him and for you. But, it's an essential dog grooming habit. Otherwise, his nails can start to grow excessively long and can start growing into the paw pad, which will then cause extreme pain and difficulty in walking.

To help you out, here are some reminders:

- Let your dog get used to you touching his feet. You can regularly play with his feet.

- Use high-quality nail clippers.

- Your dog's nails typically need clipping once in three weekly.

- Wear your dog out so the chances of him fussing over a nail-clipping session are less. You can play "Fetch", let him run around, or take him out for a walk.

- Don't rush the nail-clipping session – and don't let your dog know that you're in a hurry. Clipping one nail at a time lessens your dog's anxiety.

Ear Care Essentials

Because a dog's inner ear is twisty, there's a high chance of yeast, bacteria, and parasite to hide – and not to mention, thrive -- in it. Earwax and debris (such as tiny wooden pieces, dirt, and leaves) can enter relatively easy. Apart from that, these earwax and debris that have entered your dog's ear is less likely to escape because of his ear's natural design. Unless you take them out, earwax and debris that are inside his ears can only escape upwards.

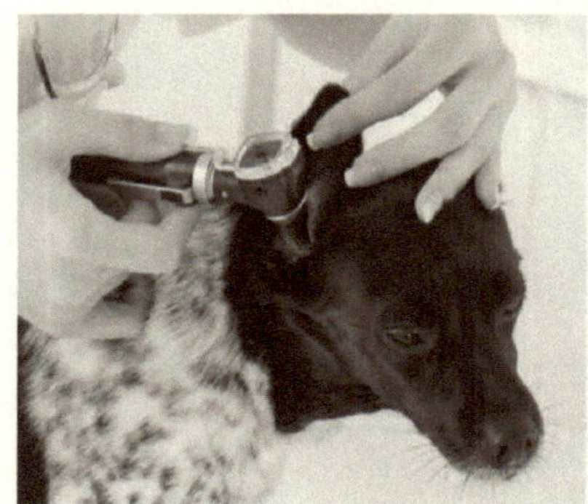

This is why you should regularly check and clean your dog's ears. Here are some tips that might help:

- Do not clean too deeply; do not forcibly insert things into your dog's ear canal. Otherwise, ear irritation can occur.

- Clean your dog's inner ears using cotton balls dampened with hydrogen peroxide, mineral oil, or a special solution for a dog's ear care. Remember, his inner ear is very delicate.

If your dog shows ear-related problems, it's recommended to consult with a veterinarian. Observe warning signs such as:

- Crusty skin
- Redness
- Swelling
- Unpleasant ear odor
- Ear discharge

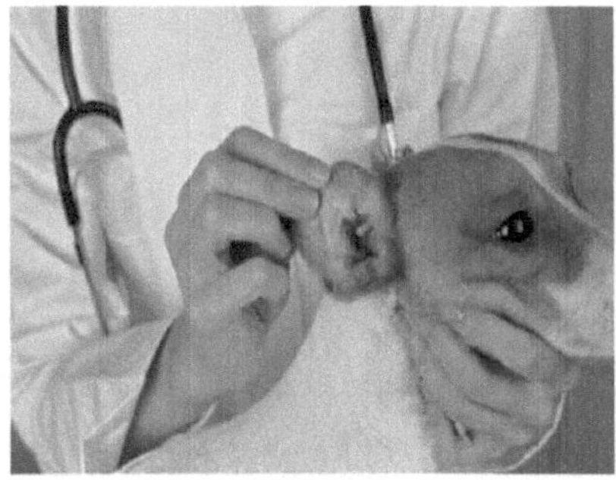

Chapter 3: Essential Grooming Tools

A properly groomed dog paints a picture of a beautiful dog. It also leads to a clean and happy one. So, if you want your dog to live a good life, investing in high-quality dog grooming tools would do the trick.

And, on a related note, before using these dog grooming tools, it's important to introduce them to your dog first. Doing so will help you in handling him in case he shows aggressive behavior. Especially if you will be using tools that can injure him due to sudden movements (such as nail clippers and trimmers), letting him familiarize himself with such tools first will lessen the chances of him injuring himself.

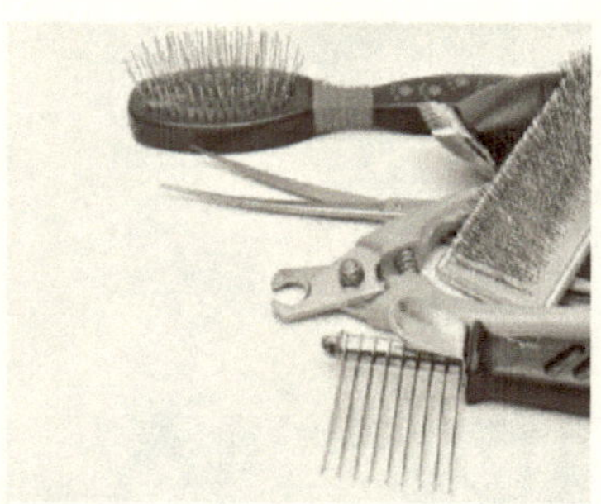

Brushes

Brushes are available in wire pin bristles (for wooly coats), versatile bristles (for typically most dog breeds), and slicker bristles (for thick hair)

Step-by-step guide on how to use the equipment:

- Step 1: First, bring your dog close to you. Hold him if he tends to run away.
- Step 2: Next, introduce the brush to your dog. Let him play with it if he wants.
- Step 3: Next, gently brush his hair in the head.
- Step 4: Next, gently, brush the hair on his body.
- Step 5: Lastly, gently brush other areas of his body.

Combs

Combes can be used for untangling knotted hair, removing dead hair, and massaging your dog's skin and are available in fine-tooth combs (for dogs with soft, silky coat), medium-tooth combs (for most dogs with any type of coat), rubber curry combs (for dogs with short hair), and wide-tooth combs (for dogs with heavy matted fur)

Step-by-step guide on how to use the equipment:

- Step 1: First, bring your dog close to you. Hold him if he tends to run away.
- Step 2: Next, introduce the comb to your dog. Let him play with it if he wants.
- Step 3: Next, start with the hair on your dog's the head. Comb his hair on the head gently.
- Step 4: Next, move on to the rest of the hair on his body. Remember to comb the hair gently.
- Step 5: Lastly, gently finish up with the rest of the hair on your dog's body.

Hair Clippers

Hair clipper are an appropriate grooming tool for trimming your dog's hair for warm months. Many hair clippers also are also available with Snap-On blades for easier use.

Step-by-step guide on how to use the equipment:

- Step 1: First, wash your dog. Then, brush his hair. This helps eliminate matted areas that can be difficult to work with.
- Step 2: Next, introduce the comb to your dog. Let him play with it if he wants.
- Step 3: Next, switch on the hair clipper and wait for a while to let your dog adapt to the noise.
- Step 4: Next, use the hair clipper in an area with hair growth. This produces a smooth clipping.

- Step 5: Lastly, use the hair clipper on areas where you want to
  clip. While you can use it as long as you can, remember not to let
  it get excessively hot. Otherwise, turn it off or use a spray-on
  lubricant.

Nail Clippers

Nail clippers are an appropriate grooming tool for clipping your dog's nails
when they grow excessively long.

Step-by-step guide on how to use the equipment:

- Step 1: First, introduce the nail clippers to your dog.

- Step 2: Next, figure out a way to let your dog stay put. You can
  use a leach, or hold him firmly. This lessens the chances of him
  escaping in case he freaks out during the nail-clipping session.

- Step 3: Next, hold your dog's paw closer to you. Ensuring that he
  is being held firmly lessens the risk of him getting injuries in case
  he freaks out.

- Step 4: Lastly, use the nail clipper to clip each one of your dog's
  nails carefully. You can clip until a white portion inside of his nail
  (with a black dot in the middle) is visible.

Toothbrush (& Toothpaste)

Toothbrushes along with toothpaste are appropriate grooming tools for
cleaning your dog's teeth and mouth.

Step-by-step guide on how to use the equipment:

- Step 1: First, prepare your dog dental care kit. You need to have
  all your grooming tools handy.

- Step 2: Next, bring your dog close to you – to where you could
  firmly hold him while you work on his mouth.

- Step 3: Next, introduce the contents of your dog dental care kit to
  your dog. Importantly, introduce his toothbrush and toothpaste
  (especially the smell) to him.

- Step 4: Next, firmly hold your dog's mouth. Then, lift its lips. This will expose the external surfaces of your dog's teeth and gums.
- Step 5: Next, gently brush his teeth using your dental tools -- as you would normally do when brushing your own teeth. Remember to clean all the way back to his molars.
- Step 6: Lastly, rinse his mouth with a generous amount of water.

Dog Scissors

A good pair of dog scissors is an appropriate grooming tool for finish styling or more precise grooming and is available in thinning shears, curved shears, and straight shears.

Step-by-step guide on how to use the equipment:

- Step 1: First, introduce the dog scissors to your dog.
- Step 2: Next, put the blades of the scissors in a thick area of your dog's coat. Remember to do this slowly.
- Step 3: Next, start cutting in that area.
- Step 4: Lastly, set aside the cut hair. You can use a brush.

De-Matting Equipment

De-matting equipment breaks up matted hair and make them more manageable and is recommended for dogs with an unruly coat.

Step-by-step guide on how to use the equipment:

- Step 1: First, introduce the comb to your dog. Let him play with it if he wants.
- Step 2: Next, brush your dog's coat to loosen the mat.
- Step 3: Next, place the de-matting equipment under matted area (with its dull side against your dog's skin).
- Step 4: Next, position your fingers between your dog's skin and the de-matting equipment. This will prevent discomfort and skin-pulling.

- Step 5: Next, slowly move the de-matting equipment through the matted area (in saw-like motions) to break up the matted area.

- Step 6: Lastly, brush through your dog's coat to collect loose hair.

Chapter 4: Preparing your dog for its grooming session

Dog grooming may be essential, but try telling that to your dog. His reaction to grooming is most likely to get away from you. No matter how sensible the idea is, he'll likely do everything in his power not to get groomed.

For him, rolling in the mud or playing with dirty items are not such bad ideas. He's happy, and for him, that matters the most. This is why you should approach the situation properly, and in a way, that works for both of you.

Handling Dogs with Anxiety

Just like people, dogs can suffer from anxiety disorders, too. Even the most harmless situations (such as you getting a new chair) can trigger him, and unfortunately, it will take hours (if not days) for him to overcome a panic attack. If you're a first-time dog parent, you may conclude that dogs tend to overreact.

And, the bigger problem is, unlike it is for people, talking to therapists is not an option for your dog. You can't simply instill "words of wisdom" to them, too. On the other hand, you can treat your dog's anxiety relatively easy.

It's a wrong move to aggravate and "force" him to behave as you would want. This will only make him more terrified and raise his aggression level to the point of barking loudly at you – or worse, he may end up biting you.

If you force him, he may start seeing you as his enemy, and if he does, he will be even more anxious and harder to handle.

So, instead of forcing him to behave in a certain way, you should do the opposite.

Here are some steps that you could follow:

- **Step 1:** First, let your dog calm down by giving him a treat. You could also pat his back while he's chewing. Not only will this lessen his anxiety, this will also promote overall comfort.

- **Step 2:** Next, give your dog another treat. This will calm him down even more, and will make him start to understand you're on his side. He will get the idea you're not an enemy and your actions will be beneficial to him.

- **Step 3:** Lastly, once you can sense your dog is in a comfortable state, tell him he's going to get groomed. Just say the words and let him see the dog grooming kit.

Remember to calm him down regularly – every pre-dog grooming session. Remember, dogs are habitual animals and their fast-learning tendencies are advantageous. If this becomes routine, your dog will start calming down (yes, all by himself) before all the following dog grooming sessions.

If your dog is difficult to handle, and refuses to calm down even after giving him a couple of treats, you could try alternatives, like:

- Use aromatherapy for dogs. Some of the essential oils that can decrease your dog's anxiety are citrus, jasmine, and valor.

- Secure your dog in a crate.

Training Your Dog to Behave Properly During Grooming

Training your dog to behave properly during grooming sessions can be challenging, but it is definitely doable. The challenge is (at least) twice as much if you have an adult dog (about 3 years and older).

This is why you should train your dog as soon as possible – while he's as young as ever. When he's about a month old, he can start following instructions. And, more likely, his young age (and his fresh mind) makes for a less challenging teaching sessions. While it's natural for him to rebel against dog grooming, he will likely be less defiant if he starts seeing the fun side in dog grooming sessions.

Here are some steps that you could follow:

- **Step 1:** First, introduce ALL dog grooming tools – the ones that you have and plan to use – to your dog.

- **Step 2:** Next, give your dog a treat as you introduce these dog-grooming tools to him once more. Remember to introduce the grooming tools individually – not as a group.

- **Step 3:** Next, use an appropriate dog grooming tool (such as a brush) to groom your dog. You can use all if necessary, but if you plan to use just one, keep the rest of the dog grooming tools in sight. Doing so lets him understand that such tools are harmless.

- **Step 4:** Lastly, reward your dog with a treat. If he feels that behaving properly can earn him a treat, he will start doing just that: behaving properly.

The key in getting your dog to behave properly during grooming sessions is regular training. During the sessions, do you your best to be understanding and patient. Just give him time to get accustomed to the idea. In addition, don't forget to reward him with a treat whenever he's successful.

In case of dog misbehavior (such as him showing untoward aggression), you should intervene. He may not easily understand the benefits of dog grooming, but you should let him understand that some actions are unacceptable.

To do this, you could say NO along with a minor punishment (such as temporarily depriving him of a treat). Avoid using force because it will only be ineffective.

Chapter 5: A Step-by-step Guide to Caring for Your Dog's Coat

Caring for your dog's coat is another essential part of dog grooming. While it seems that washing, trimming, and brushing would do the trick, dog coat care does not stop there.

Step 1: Familiarize Yourself with the Condition of Your Dog's Coat

Before anything else, learn about your dog's coat. Identify whether he has shiny, mat-free coat or a matted one. This will help you determine whether he needs basic dog coat care or a more advanced coat management.

A shiny and mat-free dog coat is a sign of a healthy dog. This means, your dog may simply need basic dog coat care, and would be satisfied with the normal management of his coat. Regularly ensuring that his coat is clean can be enough.

On the other hand, if your dog has matted coat, it's a sign that he may have (and may be developing) health problems. If you look closely at his coat, you may notice allergies, rashes, and skin conditions of sorts; that, or he may have red spots that can indicate an internal health problem.

In the case that your dog has matted coat, you need to step up and start going beyond basic dog care. Especially if he has red spots, you should let a veterinarian evaluate him. Immediately, you should clean him up and implement changes to improve his situation.

Step 2: Inspect Your Dog's Diet

Next, inspect your dog's diet. If his diet involves healthy and balanced meals, you should continue giving him the same meals because it will help keep his skin and coat healthy. In the case of an unhealthy and unbalanced diet, however, you should change the meal plans as soon as possible.

A malnourished dog can show coat problems such as a dry and flaky coat. Even if you clean his coat as needed, his poor nutrition will still get in the way of him sporting a problem-free coat. You should change his diet into a healthy and balanced one immediately because the longer he stays on that diet, the problems with his coat may worsen (and be more difficult to treat).

For your dog to sport a healthy coat, you should focus on providing dog nutrition that involve dog foods that are high in fiber, riboflavin, fatty acids (such as omega 3), protein, and calcium. You should also let your dog eat properly balanced meals, instead of feeding him the same set of meals every day.

Here is a list of foods that you should feed a dog to help keep his coat healthy:

- Apples (except the core)
- Eggs
- Green beans
- Oatmeal
- Pumpkin
- Salmon
- Sardines
- Sweet potatoes
- Tuna
- Yogurt

Step 3: Bathe Your Dog Regularly

Next is to ensure that your dog bathes regularly. Basic dog coat care does not require frequent bathing.

But, for more advanced dog coat care, you may have to bathe your dog as much as every other day. Especially if his coat is in bad condition, regular baths can help him improve.

Step 4: Brush Your Dog's Hair Regularly

Next comes the need for brushing. Whether basic or advanced, dog coat care requires regular brushing. Because it stimulates your dog's hair follicles and skin, brushing results to an increase in the production of natural skin oils, which leads to a shiny, mat-free coat.

Step 5: Improve Your Dog's Living Environment

Lastly, to keep (or make) your dog's coat healthy, you should check his living environment. Figure out his living conditions and the elements he's regularly exposed to.

If your dog usually stays outside of your home (and sleeps there), it's important to clean his space. And, while you're at it, eliminate the elements that only add clutter (such as leaves, tree barks, old newspapers, and unused rugs).

If your dog lives inside your home, that is also the case. You should let him stay in a clean and clutter-free living environment. On top of that, check any air fresheners and deodorizers that you use. If these are not dog-friendly, it's time for them to go.

Chapter 6: The Best Grooming Styles

A variety of dog grooming styles exists because the preferences of dog parents differ. While others are fine with simple dog grooming styles (in other words, so long as their dogs are clean, they wouldn't want more grooming to be done), other dog parents refuse to settle with the basics (in other words, they want more grooming after getting their dogs cleaned).

Either way, it's a plus to learn about different grooming styles to provide proper grooming for your dog, especially if you plan to engage in dog grooming for profit.

The Benefits of Basic Dog Grooming Styles

If you're a dog parent who does not want to make a fuzz about your dog's appearance, a basic dog grooming style seems ideal for you. You want plain and simple, and you want to be practical. You're not into fancy looks because these are likely to consume additional time.

Your dog is clean and healthy, and he requires less maintenance, and, for you, this is more than enough. An example of basic dog grooming is not cutting his hair too frequently. Your goal is to give him a haircut because he needs it, not because you want him to appear differently.

Other benefits of basic dog grooming are:

- It is more affordable because, usually, you wouldn't have to groom your dog frequently. You wouldn't have to invest in relatively many grooming products of sorts.
- It is favorable to your dog, especially if he doesn't want excessive grooming.
- It requires less time and commitment from you.

Why Go for Complex Grooming Styles?

However, while basic dog grooming can do the trick, there are dog parents who would like to go the extra mile. They want their dogs to look a lot better – or with more grooming work than a dog who underwent basic dog grooming. Hence, they prefer complex dog grooming styles.

Then again, complex dog grooming styles are not just about grooming for extravagance. Sometimes, a complex style is the best option, especially if a dog's previous groomer did a bad job in grooming him.

For such complex grooming styles (like the preference to dye your dog's hair a certain color) to work well, you may have to do a lot of work. Unless you maintain a certain appearance, your dog could only get improperly groomed after a while if you refuse to work on his grooming too often.

Sure, complex dog grooming styles can require more time and commitment. But, if you're willing to invest a lot of time and commitment (plus, you have enough financial resources), going for such styles shouldn't be a problem. These complex styles are also preferred by professional dog groomers, as well as dog owners who want to profit in making their dogs' appearance outstanding.

Here are some reasons to consider complex grooming for your dog:

- You often bring your dog to social events.
- You want a fancy look for your dog.
- you would want to check on your dog's health regularly.

The Choice: Basic vs. Complex Dog Grooming

After reading about basic dog grooming styles and complex dog grooming styles, you can see that both dog-grooming styles have their own set of advantages. Thus, your choice should depend on some factors such as:

- Dog breed (since some breeds require specific grooming styles)
- Age of dog (since some older dogs may require specific grooming styles)
- Personal resources (such as time, commitment, and money)

You should also consider your own preference. For example, if you want to go with complex dog grooming, you should go for it. Granted your dog's breed and age could work with that style, and granted personal resources are in place, that grooming style could work for you as a dog parent, too.

Chapter 7: Dogs with Fur Issues

Your dog's fur can hold major revelations about his health. A thinning fur, for example, is a sign that your dog is suffering from tumors. Hence, you should pay close attention to his fur at most times and groom it as necessary.

A New Odor

Some dogs smell bad. It's their "signature odor", and regardless of bathing them regularly, they will still carry that odor. In such a case, a smelly dog wearing his signature odor shouldn't be a problem.

The problem is when your dog introduces a new odor – and, more likely, it's not just annoying, it's also strong and foul. And, chances are, it's not from dirty and smelly plaything, and instead, it comes from him.

In such a case, this new odor is a sign of mange, ringworm, fungus, fleas, dry skin, parasites, or bacterial infection. So, you should always be observant of his smells.

A solution is to bathe your dog more often (such as every other day), and see if the smell goes away. In about a few minutes, the smell will disappear right after his bath, but will return hours later or as soon as he starts to sweat. On the other hand, if the smell persists, it's cue to schedule a visit to a veterinarian.

Some Conditions That Cause Issues with Your Dog's Fur

If he is losing his fur (and you can rule out other reasons), your dog may be suffering from Allergic Dermatitis. This happens if he is allergic to a new element (such as a toy, foods, home cleaning agents, soaps, or a rug).

Initially and (in the case of mild and moderate conditions), it begins with a small allergy, a bald or red spot, or a harmless rash. Once it affects a small area, it's recommended to treat it immediately. Otherwise, it can worsen by starting to spread and affect larger areas, and by then, the affected area can be difficult to treat.

A viable treatment option is to eliminate the new element that causes an allergic reaction. Once you can identify the cause, you should remove it from your dog's living environment, and sanitize the new area.

Luckily, Allergic Dermatitis is treatable easily. You can:

- Use a spray-on treatment for hot spots.
- Use an anti-itch shampoo

Hypothyroidism is also another condition that causes hair loss in dogs. This happens when your dog's thyroid produces relatively less hormones – less hormones than necessary. The challenging aspect of Hypothyroidism in dogs is being very difficult to detect.

So, if your dog is losing his fur (and you can rule out other reasons), it's recommended to send him to a veterinarian for patch testing. Once he tests positive for the condition, he will be prescribed medication.

If Allergic Dermatitis and Hypothyroidism are off the table as to the cause of fur loss in your dog, a condition called Acantosis Nigricans may be the culprit. Such condition happens because your dog's skin is darkening abnormally on top of fur issues. Only a skin biopsy can diagnose this condition.

Unfortunately, Acantosis Nigricans is not (currently) curable. But, with steroids, melatonin, anti-seborrheic shampoos, it is manageable. Bathing your dog regularly also helps.

Cushing's Disease can also be the cause of your dog's issue with his fur. This happens due to an increase in the corticosteroids in your dog's body.

This should be treated as soon as possible because its effects go beyond fur issues. This condition also results in lethargy, irrational exhaustion, and bruising.

Chapter 8: Dogs Dental Care

Dog dental care is important in dog grooming, but unfortunately, it's also one of the most neglected part. Some dog parents assume that just because their dogs' teeth (and mouth) look clean that these areas don't need care. Well, they're wrong.

Dog Dental Care 101

Just like people's teeth, your dog's teeth need cleaning, too. Otherwise, germs of sorts can accumulate inside his mouth, which can lead to tartar build-up, toothache and tooth decay, bad breath, and other periodontal diseases.

But, unlike people's teeth, your dog's teeth are less prone to dental problems – so long as you brush them regularly. And, unlike people (who could use teeth-brushing after every meal), brushing your dog's teeth once daily would suffice.

Choosing the Right Toothpaste

It's important to use a dog-friendly toothpaste and not just an ordinary toothpaste for people. Most of these dog-friendly toothpastes will also help catch your dog's interest in teeth brushing because they come in meaty flavors (such as poultry and pork). Alongside, most – if not all – toothpastes for people contain a poisonous element to dogs: fluoride.

Neither should you use other cleaning agents such as baking soda, salt, and soap. While they may seem harmless when used on people's teeth, these cleaning agents can be toxic to your dog. And, if your dog ends up swallowing the components of these cleaning agents, a trip to the veterinary hospital may be in order.

Chew Toys Help!

Chew toys promote the oral health of your dog by keeping his teeth clean. This is why it's recommended to regularly give him chew toys so long as these chew toys are safe (in other words, with dull ends and no toxic components).

But, while they seem an easy option towards his oral health (because all you need to do is just hand them to him), chew toys can also be tools that your dog will simply ignore. Like people, your dog will also not be interested in certain things. To increase the chances of him wanting to receive the chew toys from you, consider their size and your dog's size – neither too big nor too small for him.

And, apart from cleaning your dog's teeth, there are other benefits to these chew toys such as:

- They strengthen your dog's teeth by exercising the muscles in his mouth.
- They relieve your dog of boredom. They will entertain him for a few hours (or as long as he finishes these toys).
- They are appropriate tools for satisfying your dog's innate need to chew.

Chapter 9: Where to Get Your Dog Grooming Supplies

Investing in dog grooming supplies is a good choice because your dog would need high-quality tools to maintain his condition. Such grooming tools may be costlier than low-quality ones, but they are wise investments.

Besides, low-quality grooming supplies tend to be less durable. Not only that; you should also prefer these high-quality grooming tools because such tools would decrease the chances of resulting in grooming-related injuries.

What if I Prefer Homemade Dog Grooming Supplies?

Preferring homemade dog grooming supplies is an option, especially if you want to reduce expenses. Unless you want to engage in dog grooming for profit, and unless you want to be a dog-grooming professional, going for DIY dog grooming tools is not a bad idea, at all.

You can even use some of your current grooming tools (such as a brush, comb, hair and nail clippers, scissors, and de-matting equipment). Ordinary grooming tools will suffice for basic dog grooming. Ensure, however, you will use them solely for your dog.

Apart from that, be mindful of these factors:

- The length of your dog's nails
- The thickness and length of your dog's coat

On the other hand, for dog grooming products whose ingredients involve chemicals (such as dog shampoos, dog soaps, and dog toothpastes), it's safer to buy from a reputable dog store – unless, of course, you're familiar with all the chemicals that are toxic for your dog.

A Reputable Dog Grooming Supplier

If you want store-bought ones, buying your dog grooming supplies from a reputable supplier is recommended. Practically, a reputable supplier is a guarantee the dog grooming supplies are made of high-quality materials. That, and may even come with complimentary dog grooming services.

Sure, compared to going for DIY dog grooming supplies, buying supplies from reputable dog grooming suppliers is costlier. But, if you're willing to invest in your dog or maybe you want to be a dog groomer for profit, the latter is a sound investment.

Chapter 10: Extreme Grooming Makeovers

Especially if he has not been groomed for at least a few weeks, your dog could use a makeover – and an extreme one. After a makeover, he can look a lot differently (and almost unrecognizable), but usually, it's for his advantage.

The Need for an Extreme Grooming Makeover

Giving dog makeovers can sometimes be necessary. If you're simply doing a makeover for fun and for your own dog, you have all the freedom to tweak his appearance as you wish. Apart from just trimming his hair and nails, you want to (and will) dye his hair.

While giving him an extreme one is fine if you're the dog parent, but if you're not – and you're simply providing dog-grooming services – it's recommended to just go with a standard clean look. Unless the dog parents who availed of your services have approved, it's unadvisable to insist on doing an extreme makeover.

Grooming Makeovers Gone Bad

In some cases, dog parents who have sent their dogs to professional dog groomers, have gotten dismayed after a few hours. While they have given their consent, they can only resent the dog groomers who worked on their dogs.

The sad part, however, is that their dog groomers are not always the ones at fault. As mentioned, makeovers – even extreme ones -- can sometimes be necessary. The goal is to groom your dog accordingly – not to shock you, but as a means of improving your dog's quality of life. One of the best ways around this concern is not to leave your dog's side during grooming sessions.

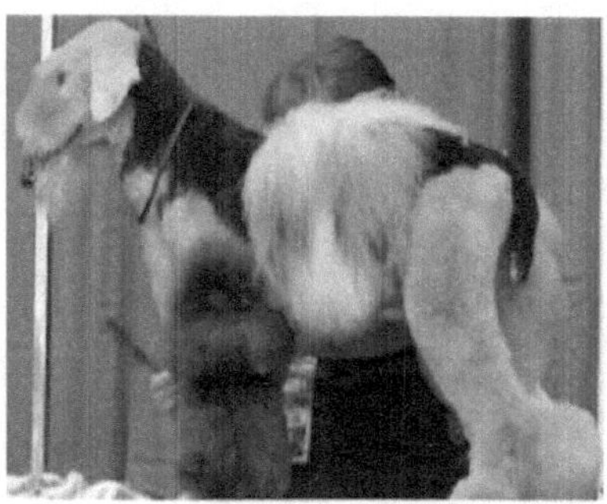

On the other hand, you can say that it's a dog groomers fault on some occasions such as:

- You clearly stated not to touch certain body parts, or you gave specific grooming instructions
- The grooming makeovers is unnecessary (such as your dog's hair was dyed pink or dog sports a haircut that resulted to his inconvenience)

Fortunately, after some time (weeks or months), your dog's appearance will start to improve despite the grooming makeover that went badly. At the very least, you know which dog grooming styles work, as well as which ones are hardly a good fit for your dog.

Grooming Makeovers That Went Well

However, while some grooming makeovers haven't gone well, situations can turn the opposite direction. In addition, of course, any dog parent couldn't be happier -- especially if the makeover significantly improved your dog's appearance and health. Even if it seems unnecessary, so long as your dog looks much more attractive in his new look, having him undergo an extreme makeover will be reconsidered.

Chapter 11: Conclusion

Thanks for purchasing this book!

I hope this book enlightened you to all the essentials about dog grooming. I hope you are (more) confident to tackle on DIY dog grooming projects. In addition, whether you will be grooming your dog for fun or for profit, I hope you succeed.

If you used to have second thoughts about dog grooming, you should be rid of these things by now. You can definitely handle the task. So long as you're committed to make it all work for the best, grooming your dog on your own is not impossible – as this book could tell.

Remember, you will be working with a dog; you will be grooming a dog. Generally, not all dogs are difficult to handle. They are smart and attentive animals who can learn to follow instructions easily.

I would really appreciate it if you would spare a moment of your time to give me a positive review on Amazon for this book.

Good luck!

* 9 7 9 8 5 4 6 4 3 0 4 5 0 *